THE WORLD OF
HORSES

COOMBE BOOKS

Of the many animals that have befriended man the horse is surely the most magnificent. It is a symbol of strength, courage and majesty. On its sturdy back have sat great warriors, monarchs and statesmen; great conquests have been made and new territory explored. Without it the invention of the wheel would have been virtually redundant and much of the land upon which man grew his own food would have remained uncultivated. It is impossible to imagine just how differently the pattern of our own history would have emerged had it not been for the hard work, patience and loyalty of the horse, and for this contribution alone we are indebted to it. Even today, as its agricultural and haulage uses draw to a close, the horse remains an important part of our society and increases our enjoyment of leisure time as the popularity of equestrian sports grows. It is flattering that such a noble beast is happy to feature so prominently in our society and the place it occupies in many peoples' lives is indispensable.

To look at the stately horse of the modern age it is hard to believe that its ancestor was little bigger than a fox. But skeletons unearthed in the Mississippi Valley in the United States show that the first horse Eohippus, that foraged the undergrowth in the Eocene forests over fifty million years ago, stood roughly one foot high. Eohippus (Greek for the 'Dawn Horse') was unique in that it had four toes on the front limb and only three on the hind, but many scientists believe that it could run as fast as the modern race horse. Its modest frame, however, was

(1) Przewalski's Wild Horse and Foal.
(2) A sleepy Arab foal nuzzles the buttercups and daisies in a sunny meadow.
(3) The stance of this Arab foal emphasises its long, gangling legs. (4) This Arab *horse displays a regal turn of the neck. (5) An appealingly fluffy New Forest foal seen on Wiverley Plain, Hampshire, England. (6) Arab mare and foal. (7) Shire foal.*

4

5

6

7

1

2

3

not suitably equipped to survive in its environment and it mysteriously disappeared. But by this time more advanced species had developed. Over millions of years these species constantly underwent change, adapting to their surroundings and developing qualities specifically designed for their survival. Eventually they evolved into Equus, the single species to which all modern horses belong. Early Equus, a sturdy dun-coloured animal now known as Przewalski's horse, travelled outwards from Eurasia establishing local breeds to the east and west. In Europe, breeds were established from the migratory horses which ranged through Asia Minor and they were also to reappear in the New World, in 1519, when the Spanish explorer Hernando Cortez, transported the ancestral horse to its original prehistoric home.

The origins of the domestic horse are less clear. All are descended from four sub-species of the original wild horse but exactly when the horse was first harnessed is not accurately known. Prehistoric man drew pictures of the early horse on the walls of his cave many thousands of years ago but it is unlikely that he did more than keep the herds for meat, milk and hides. The first horsemen were probably the barbarian nomads of Central Asia who rode hardy wild ponies. Certainly by the end of the Bronze Age the horse's potential had been realised and from then until the invention of the steam train in the 19th century, most land transport all over the world was carried out by horseback. On farms and in coalmines the horse proved equally invaluable and it is only recently that the role of the horse has changed from servant to friend. Unfortunately, so well did the horse carry out the work man asked of it that man forgot the horse's body was evolved for its own survival and not specifically for his usage. Instead of being grateful that so noble a beast should allow its skills to be used for the purpose of his own progression,

(1) Przewalski's Wild Horse and foal. (2) Arab mare and foal. (3) Three horses bask in evening sunlight. (4) This peaceful grey is seen in the Carmargue, France. (5) Group of four greys. (6) Grazing in Norway. (7) Pair of Arab fillies. (8) Arab foal. Overleaf Part bred Arab colt and mare.

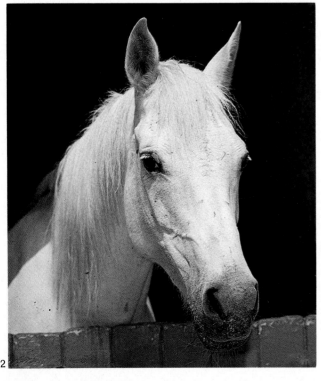

1

2

3

4

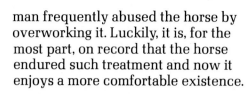

man frequently abused the horse by overworking it. Luckily, it is, for the most part, on record that the horse endured such treatment and now it enjoys a more comfortable existence.

Horses and Battle

The horse's potential on the battlefield was realised very early on. History relates that the first major victory of cavalry over the infantry was in AD 378 when the Goths defeated the Romans at Adrianople, but even before this horses were used to pull chariots. It was with the invention of javelins and bows that the need to employ the horse elsewhere in battle arose and the cavalry was established, quickly becoming an army's major striking force. By the middle of the sixth century the Great Horse of Europe, which is the ancestor of all the heavy breeds used in war, had grown considerably in size and strength and heavy armour was introduced. When

5

6

7

8

King John brought over from Europe a hundred dray stallions to combine with the English stock, the size of the horse increased further and battles became considerably more ferocious.

The invention of firearms almost totally displaced the cavalry from the battlefield and today it serves no function in modern warfare. But all over the world small cavalry units are maintained and horses are the main feature of military displays and ceremonial occasions.

(1) Pure bred Arab foal. (2) Arab horse. (3) Pure bred Arab foal seen in Sussex, England. (4) Proud cream mare and pretty foal. (5) Dun Arab mare and foal. (6) These delightful Shetland ponies contentedly munch hay on a snow-dusted hillside in Somerset, England. (7) Piebald Shetland pony. (8) An Arab foal lies at the feet of its protective mother.

Horses and Agriculture

Until the invention of machinery the horse's use in agriculture was indispensable. All farm work was carried out with its help and the transportation of goods was by horseback or horse-and-cart, with the added advantage that the horse was cheap to run – a fact which few modern machines can claim to be.

Man first discovered how invaluable the horse would be in agriculture when he used the wild horse to help him hunt. He quickly realised that if he stayed in one place and kept a few of the animals he hunted in captivity they would breed and he would no longer have to go out searching for his food. He also discovered that he could cultivate the land around him and grow his own crops and for both purposes the horse became an invaluable aid. When cattle strayed it was a simple enough task to round them up if on horseback and when the plough was invented it was eventually the horse that pulled it.

On most large farms throughout the world machines now do the work that was once done by the horse, but few are as versatile, and in many mountainous regions the horse is still the most efficient means of ploughing the land and transporting goods.

Famous Breeds

If the mating of two horses of the same kind consistently results in a horse of the same appearance, colour, height and temperament it can be said that these horses belong to a particular breed. There are numerous modern breeds that vary greatly in appearance and character, but one common feature is that they all developed from the stocky wild horse of central Asia. When and how the emergence of different breeds occurred is unclear, but it is likely that the migratory horses that travelled across Europe and Asia in prehistoric times eventually developed, broadly speaking, into two groups of horses; the hot-blooded Arab-Barbs, typified by the Arabian, and the heavier working breeds.

The Arabian, renowned for its beauty, stamina and spirited yet gentle nature is considered the monarch amongst horses. It moves

(1) Richly caparisoned horses take part in a ploughing championship. (2) Horses still play an important part in the work of many farms. (3) The proud farmer displays his trusty, and strong companion. (4) Working horses can easily be distinguished by their build. (5) Ploughing competition. (6) Ploughing with Shire horses. (7) Beautifully kitted out horse on show. (8), (9) and (10) Hard at work or on display, horses are true friends.

with a grace no other horse can match – its limbs long and slender, its small head held high with an air of superiority. First mentioned in 400 BC it is thought to have stemmed from a gift of five mares given to Muhammed by his followers. It was imported into Europe after the crusades and has remained pure bred until today. It is also the forefather of all modern light breeds. The swiftest of all breeds descended from the Arabian is the Thoroughbred, the favourite in many equestrian sports. Whilst retaining the spirit and courage of its ancestor, the Thoroughbred far exceeds it in size, speed, agility and stamina and it is thought that it can run as fast as is physically possible for any animal whilst carrying a man on its back.

Before the creation of the Thoroughbred, Europe's most famous breed was the Andalusian, a result of Oriental stock, brought over by the Moors in the eighth century, being crossed with Spanish ponies. These horses can be trained to an exceptionally high standard and they were in great demand on European battlefields during the Middle Ages. Other famous breeds have been established from it, most notably the Lippizaner. Lippizaner stallions are considered the best trained horses in the world and their exciting displays still contain many of the mediaeval cavalry exercises.

All the heavy draught breeds that are known as 'working horses', including the Great Horse of Europe, are descended from a sub-species of wild horse called the Forest Tarpan which looked similar to the modern Norwegian Dun. There are numerous draught breeds; the French Percheron, Austrian Prizganer, the English Shire which is the world's largest horse, and they come in a variety of colours. Few of these horses weigh less than a ton and their heights range between sixteen to nineteen hands. A Shire can pull up to five tons and remarkably enough has an extremely docile nature.

There are numerous varieties of ponies, in cold and warm countries. Colour, shape and temperament vary (although all display more than a hint of stubbornness); the only criterion for calling a horse a pony is that, unless it is an Arabian, it should be less than 14.2 hands in height. Usually

Since the domestication of the horse, it has played a significant role as man's partner and friend. It has been a means of transport and a war companion as well as a recreational partner in all manner of sports. Showjumper or shepherd, carthorse or thoroughbred, the horse in all its guises is a noble and intelligent animal which truly deserves our respect.

gentle, intelligent and very active, they have delightfully willing natures which make them excellent riding horses for children.

Equally good-natured but even more stubborn, the donkey also belongs to the horse family. The only major differences between the two are the half-haired tail, the upright mane and of course the larger, floppier ears, characteristics which it shares with certain other wild horses such as the zebra. Donkeys are small but sturdy and in many countries are still used to carry packs across country, especially in mountainous regions, where its sure-footedness makes stumbling a rare thing. In the paddock, if a new horse is brought in alone, the placid donkey can provide excellent companionship and a steadying influence if the horse is particularly nervous.

Horses, like most other animals, and humans, are inquisitive and they take an interest in whatever is going on around them. They are fond of company and much prefer to have other horses in the field with them.

Australia and the U.S.A.

Covering nearly three million square miles in total area, the wild and rugged plains of Australia combine to make up the largest island in the world. This is the land of bucking broncos, bareback riding and steer wrestling – the land where those ever popular television characters, the cowboys, really do exist, displaying a standard of riding that is of the very highest. Vast areas, sometimes larger

than countries, are uninhabited – the total population of Australia amounts to little over that of some of the world's capital cities – and herds of sheep and cattle roam freely within boundaries that are so wide that the grazing land available to them appears inexhaustible. The value of the horse in this massive, agricultural country is immeasurable. What better way to keep charge of an enormous herd of sheep than sitting astride the versatile, strong, reliable horse? The men responsible for looking after and rounding up the herds are called 'ringers' and live in the saddle for days on end. For the sake of comfort they adopt a riding posture very different from those who ride for pleasure and who therefore spend less time actually on the horse. They sit well back in the specially designed high pommeled saddles and so ride with their legs considerably straighter.

Named after its home state of New South Wales, the Waler is the national horse of Australia. Lack of interest in the past has rendered the horse virtually extinct twice in its history, but its future now looks more certain as its qualities are once again being taken into account. Many of the English heavy working breeds such as the Shire and Clydesdale have been imported into the country and, with equestrian sports obviously finding a popular niche in Australian society, Arabs and English Thorougbreds have been brought in as well.

The relationship between the people of Australia and their 'four legged friends' to whom they owe much of their livelihood, is a very special one. Despite the fact that many of the men spend much of their working lives in the saddle, immense pleasure is gained from being with horses in leisure time as well, not only from organised sporting activities but also impromptu races and shows. The competitors have fun and the horses benefit from an exciting, active life and owners who appreciate their value and treat them with respect and understanding.

Peace or pageantry – a horse seems at home in either circumstance. Cowboys and bucking broncoes, bareback riders and steer-wrestling horses, especially in America and Australia, can be seen as part of many colourful and exciting displays.

Horses are not native to America. The early Spanish settlers in the 16th century brought with them the noble Andalusian horses from their own country and with the help of their horses explored new territory. At first the horses were regarded with awe and suspicion by the local Indian tribes, but as the amount brought into the country increased they became accustomed to the animals and quickly learned their potential. Many were stolen and the notorious mounted Indian tribes that terrorised the Western settlers enjoyed a short, but memorable heyday.

Gradually the horses broke away from the captive environment, adapting successfully to feral life because of the vast areas of rich pastureland that covered most of the country. Eventually the Andalusian degenerated into groups of wild horses now called Mesteno or Mustangs.

In America, as in Australia, the inhabitants are indebted to the horse and it has become a major feature of their folklore. Without it, early pioneers would never have settled successfully and the 'Wild West' would have remained unexplored.

If ever you stop at a field of horses you will find that they usually come over to take a closer look. Horses sleep little, but spend a lot of time dozing—standing or lying half asleep with their eyes almost closed and their ears back. Foals need play as much as they need food and sleep as it is vital to their growing muscles and sense of coordination. Horses have a keen sense of sight and can see colours as we do! They are very perceptive to movement—an adaptation developed as a form of protection and dating back to wild ancestors.

In the Wild

Very few truly wild horses still exist. A small group of Przewalski's horses, named after the Russian explorer Colonel Przewalski who discovered them, roam the land bordering China and remote parts of Mongolia and Russia. All other horses that are called wild are actually feral; descended from domesticated breeds.

Watching any animal in its natural environment is undoubtedly the best way of understanding its basic social habits. It also proves an invaluable way of learning how to treat it if it is taken away from its natural environment and expected to live happily in an alien world such as a stable. The most basic instinct of the horse is that of the herd. A group of horses offer mutual protection, they accept leadership and are sociable animals that thrive best in the company of others. Young born into a herd quickly learn the skills necessary for survival and they also benefit from a secure environment in which they can enjoy the company of other foals. A unique social system which gives each member of the herd an order of precedence ensures that harmony is maintained and whilst an experienced mare takes charge of the overall running of the herd, the stallion keeps order and is the main protector from routine dangers.

Routine is an essential part of every horse's existence but ferals adapt their grazing and resting patterns according to the amount of food available. During the summer months grass is plentiful and the herd will graze in the morning and evening, the cooler parts of the day, choosing to rest in the afternoon when the sun is at its hottest and trouble from flies is at its worst. In winter however, grass is scarce, and any that is available contains little or no nourishment, so grazing is from the first signs of daylight through to the very last. Even then, by the time the succulent spring grass appears some of the horses may have died of starvation and the general health of the whole herd will be poor.

Foals are born in the spring when the mares have plenty of nourishing grass to provide healthy food for their infants. Up to the age of four, male foals are called colts and females fillies. Fillies are fortunate in that they

All domesticated horses belong to the same species and are descended from the Eurasian wild horse. There were however three subspecies of wild horse and in prehistoric times, man killed them for food. Few wild horses survive today. The

Mongolian or Przewalski's horse can be found on the borders of the great Gobi desert. It is a sturdy pony, dun-coloured to bay, with an erect mane and mealy muzzle. To save it from extinction breeding herds have been established in wildlife parks.

can remain with the herd they are born into for the rest of their lives, but this is not the case with the colts. There is room for only one stallion in a herd and as the colts mature they are chased away by the stallion leader to fend for themselves. Often they will form bachelor gangs with other young stallions and it is not until they are older and considerably wiser that they will challenge another for the leadership of a herd, because only stallions of equal rank will fight.

Domestic Horses

Man is one of the few animals who can adapt quickly to his environment – an environment which more often than not he changes himself. Other animals are not quite so readily adaptable and the horse is no exception.

Today, many people derive pleasure from owning their own horse, riding it and schooling it for fun, and entering gymkhanas and other shows. A stabled horse is far removed from its natural way of life and even those that have never lived in the wild will retain the same instincts of the herd existence. To own a horse it is therefore of utmost importance to understand its own particular nature and learn to treat it correctly. No horse or pony can remain in good condition and give of its best unless it is properly fed, groomed and exercised. These are the fundamental aspects of horse ownership and if carried out wrongly or not at all, the horse will deteriorate rapidly in health and personality.

Although the horse's association with man dates back some 5,000 years, few will instantly trust a human being. All horses have naturally nervous dispositions and are easily frightened by things they do not understand, are not clearly visible or make loud noises. In the wild these would be considered a threat to their personal safety and so in the stable they have to learn to be confident in their strange surroundings. A great deal of time must therefore be spent gaining your

Safety should always be a prime consideration when riding. Particularly important are the right footwear and a protective hat – neither of which restrict the exhilarating sense of freedom which comes from a gallop through the countryside or along the seashore.

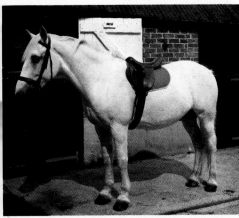

particular horse's trust, especially if it is a foal. It will not like being alone, nor will it feel safe with the various objects that surround it until it is gently introduced to them all. Kindly persuasion is the only treatment that will work with a horse. It will be instinctively terrified of dogs, noisy vehicles and anything else which is unfamiliar but if it learns to trust you, not only as a regular provider of food but also as a companion, half the battle will be won.

Many of a horse's natural attributes are to man's advantage in the early years of horse ownership. Its remarkable memory, readiness to obey and strong tendency to play 'follow my leader' make training that much easier. Once a horse has been taught a certain rule, it will remember it. It is important that its day to day life follows a regular pattern. It will look forward to seeing its owner at particular times of the day and will quickly distrust the person if these times are constantly altered. After schooling has started however, occasional breaks in training need not be a bad thing. A horse can get easily bored, which could lead to it developing a bad temper and selfish nature. More normally, any horse will have a very amenable personality and bad behaviour on its part is often a result of incompetent handling or rough treatment. As it is very sensitive to touch, punishment should be dealt out sparingly, but many horses do have a tendency to be greedy, for both food and attention. If a horse with this trait is constantly allowed to get its own way without any form of discipline it could become difficult to handle and unsafe to ride.

Understand your horse and communicate with it on the right level and it will give you its best, which is fun and exciting. If you are taking a horse into the home it really does involve a great deal of thought. There should not be odd mornings when you are late for work and are

Donkeys are also members of the horse family and have the same number of teeth as horses. Their appearance differs in the size and shape of the ears, the upright mane and the half-haired tail. Their placid nature makes them ideal companions for highly strung horses as they seem to have a steadying influence. These gentle creatures are very popular with children and will patiently plod up and down carrying small, and delighted, riders on their broad backs.

29

not able to attend to it, unless there is somebody else who the horse trusts and can do the job equally as well. A horse is a dependent animal from birth, and this dependence does not lessen as it grows older. A well looked-after horse will be happy and responsive and this should be the objective of every owner.

Creature Comforts

When grass first appeared on the plains, millions of years ago, the horse developed suitable teeth and a specialised digestive system to take full advantage of it. It is its natural food and a wild horse can live quite happily on grass alone. However, the nourishment gained from grass is only really sufficient for a horse to carry out its natural relatively lazy existence – keeping fit enough to flee from danger and to conduct other essential functions. But to do a good day's work it would not provide enough nourishment. Grass also has a high moisture content which blows out the stomach in such a way that strenuous exercise could cause problems with breathing. If a stabled horse is not a worker, four feeds a day mainly on hay should suffice. Good hay is as nourishing as spring grass and the lack of moisture in it is preferable. A horse's stomach is small, which accounts for the frequency of feeds and hay should be left in a rack in the stable at night to enable the horse to continue replenishing its stomach. The working horse needs a daily ration of grain, usually of crushed oats mixed with bran or chaff to make it more digestible, and salt, which is a vital part of its diet, should be provided in a holder. If a horse is living solely on dry food it would be a nice treat to bring some clover in for it, which grows during the summer months, and it would also enjoy a pound or two of apples or carrots (cut lengthwise for safety's sake) to vary what could become an extremely monotonous, although highly nutritious, diet.

Water is also an essential part of any animal's diet – and horses love it. It seems, when out riding, that whenever a horse comes across a pond or stream it will want to stop and drink, and many a mischievous school pony will stop and bend its

The natural time of year for both wild and domesticated horses to produce their foals is early summer when the new grass is especially lush and nutritious, providing maximum nourishment for the nursing mare. Between five and ten days from its birth, the suckling foal will also tentatively nibble at the grass, and anything else it can pick up in its mouth! Its natural inquistiveness will lead to a thorough investigation of its surroundings.

head to take long, thirst quenching sucks of water for an interminable length of time, stubbornly resisting any attempts to get it moving again. A popular myth which surrounds horses and their drinking habits is that they should never be allowed to drink except before a feed. But this idea does date back to the days when horses were only taken out for a drink once or twice a day and so drank heavily all in one go. Certainly if a horse is allowed to drink a large amount after a feed it may get indigestion and it could be quite serious if the feed contained grain which swells in the stomach. It is also true that a wild horse will sometimes only drink once a day, but this is due to the high moisture content of the grass which is released slowly inside the body. It is perhaps not commonly realised just how much a working horse, if left to its own devices, will actually drink in one day. The amount does vary according to the climate but it will seldom be less than five gallons a day and some will drink as much as fifteen gallons. Fresh water (a horse will instinctively know if it is tainted and will avoid it however thirsty it may be) must therefore be offered in a bucket frequently, especially before each feed.

SHELTER is a comfort that is close to every horse's heart. An intense dislike of cold winds and heavy rain will send a horse off quickly in search of a protected area and in the summer constant irritation from flies may restrict it to shaded areas to escape the insects. A wild horse is fairly adept at protecting itself from the elements. Forests, gullies, even a single tree all provide some sort of shelter and in a herd horses will co-operate with one another in fending off flies by standing nose-to-tail side by side. Perhaps though, this is one area where man does have a lot to offer the horse. A warm, dry stable or even a shed in the paddock will not be refused, and carefully applied ointment to help keep the flies away will certainly be greatly appreciated.

SLEEP – Although it seems an impossibility to us, a horse really does sleep standing up. Its head will often nod contentedly as it rests and it will wake up and continue grazing a short while later, apparently refreshed. Unlike other grazing animals a horse appears to need quite a lot of sleep, sometimes as much as seven hours in a full day. If it feels relatively safe from danger and the weather is warm it will often stretch out fully and have a slightly longer, deeper sleep, but it is always on the alert and will wake up at the slightest noise ready to flee immediately if necessary. Sleep is vital to a foal. It is the time, as with any infant, when most development takes place and it will stretch out full length on the ground falling into a deep sleep while its mother stands close by to protect it.

Horses At Play

All animals play. But it is not always easy to discriminate between 'play' and keeping fit, especially with adults. We may go swimming or play tennis in our leisure time but would not class these activities as play, even though they are enjoyable pastimes. A horse may canter round a field or kick the stable door for exactly the same reasons but we would almost certainly construe it as 'play' because it is not directly related with feeding, sleeping or grooming. Youngsters undeniably play, but even this is a vital way of learning skills that are required in adulthood as well as a means of establishing friendships, which are an important feature in the

A golden horse with a silver tail – it could only be a Palamino. Palamino is a colour rather than a breed and consequently the horse can be of any size. Arabians themselves are often Palaminos, as are several types of pony.

1

2

5

3

6

horse world. Many of the antics that foals indulge in enable them to find out the limitations and capabilities of their own bodies. An insatiable curiosity, which is shared by most youngsters, means that they will constantly be investigating their surroundings and, not content with just sniffing and circling small objects in an effort to identify them, will often try to pick them up and chew them, inevitably spitting them out again.

A foal on its own in a stable is not usually a happy sight. It will get easily bored and lonely without other foals or at least its mother to play with and will often amuse itself for hours by trying to stamp on its own tail or kick at the stable door just for the satisfaction of hearing the noise it makes.

Communication

It is only recently that we have realised just how important the powers of body language are. The remarkable way in which all animals, none of which possess such extensive means of vocal communication as we do, convey a variety of signals and emotions to one another that we cannot hear and often cannot even see, is all body language – a combination of postures and automatically produced chemicals that are instantly picked up by the one, or however many animals they are directed at. Horses use a great variety of facial expressions and physical gestures to make themselves understood. Nibbling the skin of another horse is a display of affection whereas baring the teeth and flattening the ears, a gesture most often seen between two stallions, is a sign of aggression.

The secretion of certain chemicals, most of which we cannot smell, plays a large part in mating and accounts for the fact that in the majority of mammals other than man, there appears to be very little of what we would actually call 'courtship'. The process of mating seems to be a very casual one with any preliminaries

A bright orange-brown horse with a mane and tail of roughly the same colour is known as a chestnut (7). Chestnut horses very often have patches of white on them, particularly on the face or legs. A small patch between the eyes is called a star and a streak from forelock to nose, a blaze.

virtually non-existent. This can be attributed to the means of communication by pheromones. Pheromones are naturally produced chemicals which greatly affect the behaviour of the animal and elicit certain responses from other members of the same species. By their production a stallion knows, therefore, when a mare is in season.

Mares And Foals

A foal endears itself to everyone. Only hours after birth, awkward legs struggle feebly to support the small fluffy frame and the foal will totter after the mother wherever she goes. With its soft-rounded muzzle and inquisitive nature – its face keenly observing every new event that occurs – few people can resist trying to stroke and feed one of these little creatures.

A mare carries her foal for about eleven months so it is born at a very advanced stage, able to walk soon after birth. In the wild this is of vital importance as the herd are constantly moving from one grazing area to another and if a foal was born totally helpless then its chances of survival in that particular environment would be slim. The following instinct, which appears to be innate in horses, is also vital just after the birth of a foal in helping to establish the parent-child bond which is of such importance in the early months. Mother and baby will learn to recognise the shape and smell of one another and eventually a mare will respond only to the cries of her own baby and similarly a foal will learn to react only when it is called by its own mother.

Naturally, horses are perfectly capable of foaling successfully in the wild with no human help whatsoever. This has been done for millions of years. But more often than not feral herds are kept a check on and the mares are taken from the herd when they are ready to foal and given the safety of a stable. A field shelter will suffice but if the birth is impeded a mare will quickly need expert attention. A foal is usually born after

The monarch among horses is generally considered to be the Arab. It is renowned for its elegance and beauty, and spirited yet gentle nature. It is the oldest and purest breed in existence today. In its native land, the Arabian peninsula, it has been pure-bred for over a thousand years!

a few hours labour and, if it is to survive, the birth must be quick. It will normally be released from the membranes and licked dry by the mare so that it is standing up and suckling within half an hour. Sometimes the afterbirth will not come away or the mare will be too weak to attend to the new-born so professional help, preferably the vet, must be sought.

For the first day or two, depending on the weather, a mare and her foal should be kept indoors and the mare should have access to plenty of rich, nourishing food. The foal will learn many basic skills by copying its mother and will be grazing with her only a few weeks after birth. Weaning takes place after about six months, although if the mare is allowed to remain with her foal she may continue to suckle it through the first winter until the appearance of the succulent green grass the following spring. Even if the foal is of a hardy breed it is advisable to keep it in a stable for that first winter if possible. Food is scarce and it is difficult for a horse to remain in good condition without travelling far and wide to find sufficient food.

In its natural environment a male foal, or colt, will remain with the rest of the herd until it is about four years old. It will then be chased away by the herd stallion until it is mature enough to look after a herd of its own. Females, or fillies, can stay with the herd for the rest of their lives.

A foal brought into the home should not be less than six months old unless it is still with its mother. If it has come from a free-living herd it will not only be lonely but frightened and unhappy in the sudden change of surroundings. If there are no other horses, or even a donkey or goat to keep it company for the early years of its life, a great deal of time should be devoted to it, earning its trust and providing very necessary friendship. Normally, an intensely curious nature and enjoyment of human attention

All modern light breeds of horses are related to the Arab, whose most distinctive feature must surely be its proud and graceful manner. The head is small and carried high and tapers from a broad, intelligent forehead to a small, delicate muzzle. The prominent eyes are large and expressive, the limbs are fine with a clean line, the coat is silky and the tail set high. The animal moves with a grace no other horse can match, but it also has tremendous speed and endurance over long distances.

will help it to adapt to its new environment. It derives great pleasure out of life and the more it is handled correctly, the more it will reward you with its trust and share with you its fun-loving nature.

Sporting Horses

Man and beast share many basic instincts, not least of which is a competitive nature. Both like to prove strength, courage and endurance over others and this is the desire which has led to sport being one of man's major leisure pursuits – and the involvement of animals, particularly horses, in it.

From the moment man first rode the horse, a race must have taken place. In Europe history dates the first equestrian sports to the times of the Roman Empire. The Romans loved sport although theirs was considerably more cruel than the

sport of today. As they spread through Europe establishing leadership in various countries they built hippodromes in which horsedrawn chariots raced speedily around. But the breed of horse used at that time was not specifically designed for fast running and it was not until the Arabians brought their own hot-blooded stoock into Europe, and they combined with the local breeds, that the standard of racing was raised. It was the cross-breeding

Horse racing is big business all over the world. Large prizes are offered, competition becomes fiercer all the time and, somehow, the horse gets faster and faster! Horse racing is a thrilling spectacle, wherever it takes place.

1

2

3

4

5

6

7

8

9

A horse with a more or less white coat is not called a white but a grey (6) and (8). Greys occur in many breeds from Arabs and Thoroughbreds to mountain breeds and Shetland ponies. Some greys appear nearly white, some attractively dappled, and some so dark that they are known as blue roan. Not all greys are born that colour–some are born almost black but are almost white when grown, such as the wild Carmargue horses in eastern France.

of the Arabian and the English breed that produced the most famous of all racing horses – the Thoroughbred.

Today flat racing and steeplechasing have a large public following. The first flat race in England was said to have been in 1174 during the reign of Henry II and it was probably run in heats over a distance of four miles, as were the majority of early races. But this length of run quickly exhausted horses and rarely gave the public the excitement of a fast finish. Gradually the distance was reduced and in modern races many of the Classics are run over a mile and a half or two miles. In Britain several classic races are run each year, including the English Derby, regarded as the greatest test for a three-year-old over one and a half miles, the Oaks and the St Leger. All three were first run in the latter part of the 18th century. Racing is also a popular sport elsewhere in the world. Australia and New Zealand have particularly good reputations and breed excellent

horses. France now holds an eminent position in the racing world and the Poules d'Essai and Prix Royal are just two of the races in which top class riders compete.

The origins of the steeplechase, of which one of the most famous is the Grand National, date back to the days when the English countryside was considerably more rugged than it is today and casual races were organised between private individuals, often to settle a dispute over property or finance. The race ran between one village and the next, probably starting from one church steeple with the finishing point at the church steeple of the neighbouring village. These rides were across open country and involved jumping hedges, streams and gates to reach the finishing point by the quickest route. Later on, the races were arranged on a circular route so that the starting and finishing points were the same or nearby. Today, although point-to-point races are still held in country areas, steeplechasing itself is a highly organised activity held on an enclosed track and supervised by the National Hunt Committee. Artificial jumps which, excepting water jumps, must be at least 4ft 6ins high, test the horse's ability and endurance and the minimum length of a race is two miles, with twelve obstacles or more strategically placed at various distances along the course.

In both flat racing and steeple-chasing, the financial aspect is now enormous. Winners of the Classics stand to collect big prize money and the increasing demand for good quality horses has led to high prices being paid for potential winners. Combined with this is the undeniable entertainment value of these sports and the resulting growth of the betting industry which now has a multi-million pound turnover every year.

Another popular equestrian sport is Polo – one of the fastest team games in the world and probably the most masterful. The name Polo is derived from the Tibetan word 'pulu' meaning a ball, and it is most likely that the game itself originated in Persia and India many centuries ago, where it was played on any open patch of ground with rules varying from district to district. The British Regiment, stationed in India in the 19th century discovered that polo was not only an enjoyable game, but an excellent way of teaching young cavalry officers good horsemanship. In 1868 the first match in England was played on Hounslow Heath. The ponies used were small – about 12^1/$_2$ hands high, and the rules were sketchy. Today the game, as with all equestrian sports, is highly organised and exciting to watch. It involves two teams of four who must remain in the saddle whilst hitting a small ball with a mallet from a galloping pony with an opponent constantly attempting to thwart the procedure. Points are scored by hitting the ball between the correct goal posts set at either end of a grass pitch three hundred yards by two hundred yards in size. A good polo pony, now much larger than the originals used on Hounslow Heath, is difficult to train and therefore expensive to buy. It is not mature or strong enough to train until the age of five after which it takes a year to teach it the game and a further year of using it in minor matches before it is ready to compete in the more important games.

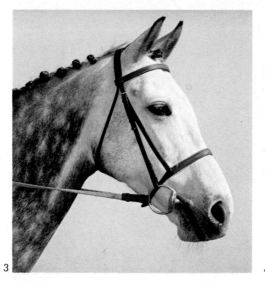

Trotting (2) is a form of light cart racing which is popular in America, Australia and Russia although it has never really caught on in Britain. It can be a very exciting spectacle and it requires great skill.

8

9

7

10

Show-jumping

Show-jumping is a relative newcomer to the equestrian sporting world. Towards the end of the 18th century it was referred to in a French cavalry manual but it was not until the 1860's that organised show-jumping events were held.

It is a popular sport, open to adults and children and fun to watch, especially at professional levels. Numerous gymkhanas are held every year in which jumpers of all standards can compete against others of similar achievement, whilst organised professional competitions are held for the experienced jumpers.

It is wrong to assume that horses naturally jump to the height required of them in the professional show ring. All animals enjoy jumping – and some can jump higher than others – but a real show-jumping horse must have the ability to consistently clear six foot fences and so is a highly specialised individual in the equine world. Temperament is also an important factor in whether a horse has the qualities of a champion, and a great deal of time and patience is needed in sorting out the potentials from the non-starters.

The popularity of the sport can be attributed to a number of things. If the fences are of a height that require horses to give of their best to jump them successfully, excitement can build up quickly. Clear rounds are possible but so are mistakes and the

Show jumping horses are very specialised individuals which must be capable of regularly clearing six-foot fences as well as having a steady temperament. Long hours of patient training, and expert riding, are essential if a horse is to reach its potential.

tension is high. It is also an easy competition for everybody to judge. Four faults for a fence down, three for the first refusal, six for the second and elimination for the third. In the event of several riders having achieved a clear round the overall winner may have to be decided by completing a further round 'against the clock'. There are basically four types of fence; the upright, the pyramid, the parallel and the staircase, and each should be designed to encourage a horse to jump to the best of its ability and not to trap it.

A three-day event, or Eventing, is closely connected with show-jumping, but many consider it to be a more thorough test of both horse and rider. The same mount is ridden throughout, and the three days consist of dressage on the first, cross-country, which is often the most rigorous section on the second, and show-jumping on the last day.

Haute Ecole could be considered the equestrian contribution to the art treasures of the world. A varied display of horses trained to an exceptionally high standard, it represents classical horsemanship at its most perfect and is pure delight to the eye.

In Italy, a little over four hundred years ago, Count Cesar Fiaschi established an advanced school of horsemanship with horses imported from Spain. Word of the school soon spread throughout the world and many famous monarchs, including Henry VIII were taught riding skills by Masters of the Horse from this school. By the time the Austrian Empire was at its highest a magnificent riding hall had been built in Vienna – the Spanish Riding School – to which riders from all over the world travelled to study methods of advanced training. Today it is still the most famous centre of Haute Ecole.

To a large extent the high standard of training achieved amongst the horses is due to their breed – Lippizaners, descended from the Andalusian horse and first bred for royal use. Only stallions are used in

Television coverage has done a considerable amount towards popularising the sport of show jumping. It is now watched by many people who have never ridden a horse and have no intention of doing so!

the Spanish Riding School and they
mature slowly, leading active lives for
many years. At the age of four,
training begins under the Riders of
the School and takes years to
complete. Each individual horse is
noted for its own particular talent for
various movements and will be
specially trained in these aspects for
display to the public. To the
accompaniment of music by Chopin,
Mozart and other composers,
spectacular demonstrations are
staged. Intricate patterns are woven
by groups of perfectly choreographed
horses under the glittering lights,
all performed with superb grace.

It may perhaps be thought that the
existence of the Spanish School is not
of particular relevance to ordinary
riders. But riding at any level is an art,
and all artists must have something to
aspire to – an ultimate goal which
represents perfection in that field.
The Spanish Riding School is that.

In all sporting events involving
horses it becomes apparent that a
high degree of training is required.
This training, far from deviating from
any natural abilities that horses
possess, nurtures them to produce
remarkable results. Driving is a sport
which is enjoying increasing
popularity and is somewhat set apart
from the others in that a well trained
carriage horse has to overcome a

*A riding horse that does not belong to any recognised
breed but somehow is of a definite type is known, in
Britain, as a hack. Colour is irrelevant but height and
temperament are of the utmost importance. High on the
list of attributes for a good riding horse are grace, intelligence
and willingness, and these can be detected at an early age.*

very basic instinct; its innate fear of being followed by something it cannot see, which in this case is the carriage, coach or gig that it is harnessed to. Harnessing several horses together for the purpose of pulling a vehicle happened early on in the domestication of horses, Greek and Roman charioteers probably being amongst the first to employ them this way. By the 18th century riding in a coach and four was a pleasurable and extremely fashionable mode of transport and today driving is popular all over the world not only as a sport but as a recreation. The horses, beautifully groomed and colourfully adorned, are trained to obey a variety of command signals and display great intelligence in allowing room for the carriage when turning through a gate. Competitions include riding rallies, scurry races and even a three-day event which is based on the pattern of the mounted one.

Hunting

The origins of hunting, the most controversial of all equestrian activities, lie in the green, pastoral American states of Virginia, Maryland and Pennsylvania, which were amongst the first to be colonised by the British. Public attitude towards the sport is almost invariably strong and can be split into two basic opinions: those who are pro the sport and those who are violently opposed, to the extent of engaging in bitter quarrels which often result in ambushing hunts. However, neither of these arguments concern the use of the horse in this activity, and there can be little doubt that a hunting party, with its magnificent horses, their riders clothed in scarlet, surrounded by a pack of excited baying hounds, is a colourful spectacle which recreates the atmosphere of a by-gone era.

In the breeding of horses specifically for hunting, Britain has not been as prolific as Europe, where there has been a greater degree of systematic selection of breeding stock. As a result the only real criterion that

Whether or not we consider hunting a desirable sport, there is little doubt that it makes a colourful and exciting spectacle. The full regalia of scarlet coat, polished boots and hunting horn echoes a strong tradition, as does the pomp and pageantry of Britain's mounted horseguards.

exists for a horse being classified as a hunter seems to be that it is actually used for hunting, regardless of its shape, size and colour. Ideally a hunter should be of a reasonable height and should be partially Thoroughbred – not only to give it agility and intelligence but, perhaps most importantly of all, tremendous stamina.

Police Horses

Many of the duties that were carried out by the first mounted police in 1763 are now undertaken by motorised vehicles such as cars, helicopters and motor cycles, but there are still many aspects of police work for which the horse is invaluable. For controlling large crowds and leading processions no vehicle can provide such gentle yet imposing force and perhaps just the sight of a policeman astride so great an animal in itself acts as a deterrent. One obvious feature which qualifies a horse for police work is its size – few small ponies could have such impact on a large crowd. But size alone is not enough. These horses must have the intelligence to be trained to a very high standard. They must learn to overcome many basic fears and not flee from loud noises, confused crowds and hazards such as smoke and fire. At training school they are introduced to these various things and patiently taught to walk quietly and maintain a controlled calm in any situation. Above all they must not panic. The mount, when dealing with such specialised horses, must be highly trained in how to handle them, so that a special relationship of mutual trust exists between horse and rider.

The Farrier

All horses, in whatever walk of life, from the riding pony to a top class show-jumper, need constant care and attention. For medical matters the most qualified person to consult is the vet, but practically anything else concerning the equipment of the horse can be handled by a farrier. Until recently few towns and villages were without their local 'smithy' but the outbreak of the Second World War brought about increased

Man has a unique and very special relationship with the horse, a relationship which has grown steadily since the animal's domestication. It has held a special place in many of man's early cultures and also in the realm of art, where it has inspired artists and sculptors throughout the centuries, all over the world.

mechanisation in order to meet the demand for home-grown produce. Farriers found that their particular skills were required less and less and were eventually forced to find work elsewhere. As a result the craft became in grave danger of dying out. Today, with the pleasures of riding rediscovered and an increase in the amount of horses being bred, the farrier is once again in great demand. Unfortunately few are to be found as it takes years to learn the trade to a high standard, and those who are working are usually too busy to take on an apprentice and devote the time necessary for training. But however far must be travelled to find a blacksmith, it is essential that a horse is attended by one several times a year, preferably once a month. A horse's feet are of the utmost importance and loose shoes, cracked hooves and splinters can cause untold damage, possibly leading to permanent lameness. Regular inspections of the feet, trimming and shaping of the hooves and re-shoeing are therefore essential from time to time. Shoeing a horse is not as painful as it may appear to the observer. The hooves are cleaned with knives and filed down before a shoe is heated until red-hot and held against the hoof so that any irregularites which remain are shown up by charring. The shoe is then shaped to fit and attached with nails to the hoof.

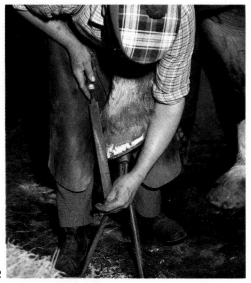

These days, a good farrier is not very easy to come by, but he is essential to the wellbeing of a horse (2). A horse should really be attended to once a month as its feet are of paramount importance. It is not simply a question of replacing an old, worn shoe, but of trimming and shaping the hoof and inspecting it for any problems. Nowadays, several farriers operate a travelling service.

6

First published in Great Britain by Colour Library Books Ltd.
© 1987 Illustrations and text: Colour Library Books Ltd.,
    Guildford, Surrey, England.
Colour separations by Llovet, S.A., Barcelona, Spain.
Printed and bound in Barcelona, Spain by Cronion, S.A.
ISBN 0 86283 244 6
COLOUR LIBRARY BOOKS